The Social Worker's Practical Pocket Guide to
Equity, Family Preservation, and Permanency

The Social Worker's Practical Pocket Guide to Equity, Family Preservation, and Permanency

10 Strategies to Practicing Cultural Humility and Trauma-Informed Care

Dr. Keisha Clark

The Social Worker's Practical Pocket Guide to
Equity, Family Preservation, and Permanency

DEDICATION

I dedicate this book to the social workers who genuinely want to "get it right" and make it right with families. Also to the families who deserve humanity, dignity, liberation, and justice.

CONTENTS

The Social Worker's Practical Pocket Guide to Equity, Family
Preservation, and Permanency

How do you expect a 16 year old to decide who and what she wants to be when she grows up? I was wired to solve problems and boss people around I would guess. Assigned as a peer assistant in high school, I mediated conflicts between my peers. I imagine I was a good communicator from that experience. I was also the student who would deliver the morning announcements over the PA system. Last, I sang in talent shows, so I was no stranger to being an extrovert. Psychology, criminal justice, and leadership in organizational management were my chosen fields of study in college. These choices led me into the field of social services and I have worked for the Health and Human Services Agency in New Orleans, Hawaii, and San Diego. San Diego County gave me my first experience at being a social worker to my surprise because I didn't have a degree in social work or previous experience as a social worker. I knew I was up for the challenge especially because I was really interested in reducing disproportionality of children who looked like myself. I knew I could do the job differently than it had ever been done. My track record speaks for itself; zero removals and 100% permanency. That means, I did not have to take any children into custody during my tenure there. As caseloads became unbearable, I started to feel the weight of it all. Single without kids afforded me the time to spend on family engagement in the field. Even I had a breaking point I suppose. Someone asked me how long I had been doing this type of work, and it dawned on me that I had been in the trauma field for 15 years and I was only in my early thirties. Half my life, not adding that I am a part of a cultural group that carries generational trauma and I am a Hurricane Katrina survivor. The families assigned to me fell into three categories: Refugee, Mexican border, and Commercial Sexual Exploitation of Children (CSEC). I realized that this career choice would not be sustainable, so I began searching for another path that would allow me to

reduce my trauma footprint and be fulfilling. That search
led me to education
and training. I landed a position training social workers in a
government agency and educating social workers in a
university setting as faculty. Those experiences led me to
where I am now; leading the Child Welfare Services Office
of Equity for San Diego County. I wrote this guide
especially for you to equip you with my lessons learned
from the field.

The Social Worker's Practical Pocket Guide to Equity, Family
Preservation, and Permanency

"You never really understand a person until you consider
things from his point of view—until you climb into his skin
and walk around in it." **Harper Lee**

The Social Worker's Practical Pocket Guide to Equity, Family
Preservation, and Permanency

1 ACKNOWLEDGE THE 4 P'S (POWER, PRIVILEGE, POSITION, PLATFORM)

The first thing you want to do before you leave the office after reviewing the case file is to **Acknowledge the 4 P's (Power, Privilege, Position, Platform).** Repeat this step as you're driving up to the home in the government issued car or your personal vehicle and again as you're walking towards the residence just to be sure.

When I would walk up to a person's home I would remind myself that I have power that they don't possess. I have the **power** to remove their child. That would make anyone feel disempowered. There is a power dissonance here. I can level the playing field by empowering the family and sharing power working together to offer choices.

I would next acknowledge my **privilege**. As a Black woman, it may be hard to think about what privilege exists, however, I have the privilege of knowing their personal otherwise confidential information. They don't know anything about me. In fact, we go to great lengths to ensure that they don't. Our license plate is set to private as well as our social media accounts. Transparency is critical here as we must both expose some vulnerable parts of ourselves. I may share that I'm a Hurricane Katrina survivor. What other privileges may you have?

What **position** do I hold? One of authority. I have been deputized. Appointed as a deputy to carry out enforcement duties. I may also be in a position of complicity with an entity that has caused harm to my own culture and

community. This induces secondary trauma and impacts my
decision making.

Last, the **platform** I hold is a powerful one. I can use it
to create barriers or to advocate. Which one will you
choose? Remember that this is not personal and you are not
representing yourself rather a governmental entity whose
reputation precedes itself.

2 EXPECT CROSS-CULTURAL COMMUNICATION

Expect Cross-Cultural Communication. There once was a tragic incident of an East African man who was experiencing a mental health crisis and was killed by police because they did not understand the way he was communicating. I served on a committee that wanted to address what needs to happen to prevent this from occurring again. We decided that law enforcement needed more training on encountering individuals experiencing mental health crises and people of different cultures. A Latina Doctora stood up and demonstrated with her hands gesturing wildly and said, "Just because I communicate with my hands doesn't mean I'm a dangerous threat." This made me think of all of the refugee families I encountered who communicated very differently when they were afraid, angry, and confused. They also communicated very differently than the way I communicate as a southerner from New Orleans. When I encountered someone who opened their door and met me with yelling, profanity, and even visceral gestures, I calmly assured them that I would probably communicate the same way if I knew someone at the door had the authority to remove my child from my home. My precious treasure. I would follow that up by saying,

"You must really love that child, I have a suspected child abuse report, suspected means anyone could have called, your sibling or partner if they are angry, I'd really love to hear your side of the story, do you mind if I step inside to protect your privacy and confidentiality from the neighbors?"

This example demonstrates cultural humility and trauma-informed responsiveness and can disarm and de-escalate the person you are engaging with. I've also had persons of a different culture not look me in the eye or prefer to talk to me through their security gate before granting me access to their home. Remember to be patient when building trust and rapport. Be sure to not label someone's behavior or responses as negative because they are not defined by traditional Western standards. Some cultures are louder and more expressive than others and that's quite alright. Expose yourself to more diverse cultures so that you'll be comfortable when engaging.

3 RECOGNIZE COMPLICITY IN SYSTEMS OF INEQUITIES

Recognize Complicity in systems of inequities. Oxford defines complicit as involved with others in an illegal activity or wrongdoing. Many organizations have acknowledged that systemic racism is rampant, apparent, overt, and covert in every system. With this knowledge, guess what? We have to admit to our complicity in being employed by a system riddled with inequities. That is a difficult yet necessary acknowledgement so that we can do the work of identifying and dismantling systemic inequities. Newsflash, I grant you permission to share this with the families you serve. They most certainly will appreciate your psychic ability to read what is on their minds and will put them at ease that you understand that the system isn't perfect. So let's take off the mask and bask in humanity with the families we serve. The families you serve may even want to dialogue further about it and share pertinent information about themselves, family dynamics, and cultural considerations that are already extremely important to your case assessment. Once we understand our role in these systems, we can work more effectively to disrupt them and also become co-conspirators with others.

Say it with me:

"I work for a system that perpetuates inequities in tandem with that of other interdependent systems. I am also empowered to creatively and critically find solutions to complex and competing priorities alongside families who are the experts of their own lives."

There, you said it, now breathe, doesn't that feel better...

The Social Worker's Practical Pocket Guide to Equity, Family
Preservation, and Permanency

4 NORMALIZE APPROPRIATE REACTIONS

Normalize appropriate reactions. What is the appropriate reaction when touching a hot stove? Some may yelp, move their hand away quickly, or even curse. All appropriate right? I'm always stomped by my colleagues who don't seem to grasp that the families we serve are being asked to comply with systems that have mistreated, damaged, injured, and killed their culture/community for generations. The families' responses to our attempts to "serve" them are justified. In the majority of our ill-attempts to serve, we end up dictating and perpetuating more of the same punitive actions that contribute to an array of social determinants. We wield more punishment when we are met with appropriate reactions. We also inadvertently invite families to be dishonest throughout the process to align with Western values that are disingenuous.

When you encounter a family reacting appropriately, acknowledge and validate their appropriate response. Assure the person that you're willing to adjust to their comfort level. Some things I offered were to allow them to choose the meeting place, meet in the car, on the porch, outside, etc. I viewed a training video that highlighted people from the Middle East and their distrust of government officials. It focused on their facial expressions, namely eye contact when being questioned by authorities. A Cambodian family I encountered also exhibited non-western eye contact. When you observe an appropriate reaction that signals fear, confusion, and even anger, let the person know what you are sensing, ask them if you're correct, and if so , how can you assist in putting them more at ease to have a conversation.

The Social Worker's Practical Pocket Guide to Equity, Family Preservation, and Permanency

"It's all right to tell a man to lift himself by his own
bootstraps, but it is a cruel jest to say to a bootless man that
he ought to lift himself by his own bootstraps." ~ *Dr.
Martin Luther King Jr.*

5 BE TRANSPARENT AND AUTHENTIC ABOUT CULTURE

Be transparent and authentic about culture. There is nothing like having to hide who you truly are when having a conversation with someone and trying to get to know them better. I found when I was open about my culture through a two-way conversation, I received more than enough information to conduct a balanced assessment. Think about it, would you want to give someone information about yourself when they have shared nothing about themselves. Stephen Covey shares in his book, The Speed of Trust that you must extend trust before someone will trust you. When you encounter someone who appears to be of your same culture, it's okay to acknowledge that. You might ask questions about differences you may have even though you belong to the same culture/community. When you encounter those who do not share your culture, immediately acknowledge that.

This is what I used to say:

"I'm from New Orleans, La. You probably hear my southern accent. I consider myself a Black/African American woman. What is your background? I don't know much about that culture/community. Can you tell me more about it?"

When encountering a Muslim family, I respectfully asked about their hijabs because some days they would wear it and other times they wouldn't and certain members never wore it. I also asked what the impressions in the community are if you choose not to wear one. They happily obliged my inquiry because I was coming from a humble, respectful, and genuinely curious place. Also, I believe when I would wear my cultural adornments such as African head wraps and colorful patterned clothing, families would sense my comfortability in my own culture and thereby was granted permission to be their full selves.

6 KNOW WHO YOU REPRESENT (GOVERNMENT)

Know who you represent. When showing up to a family's home, I would always remind myself that the person they are about to meet is not Keisha. They don't know me, they are very familiar with the employer I represent, and the reputation precedes me. Some of the strategies I used to combat the negative association and diffuse any challenging behaviors were to use open body language and a polite smile, greet the person with the salutation preferred (handshake, bow, etc.), ask how they are doing today, introduce myself without my title or badge, and craft my reason for being there in a strengths-based trauma-informed way.

For example:

"I see that you don't have any past child welfare history, you must have been doing a great job parenting, is there something that happened recently that have caused some changes?"

It's okay to name the elephant in the room as well by letting the person know that you're aware that your organization does not have the best reputation, but you are committed to preventing family separation and strengthening family's wellbeing through supportive services. You can also request that the family give you an opportunity to earn their trust. It was also my responsibility to dress the part, the more "official" you appear, the more you look as if you align with traditional practices of governmental agencies.

7 OBSERVE WHAT'S STRONG -VS- WHAT'S WRONG

Observe What's Strong -vs- What's Wrong. This is the hallmark Trauma-Informed Care Practice phrase. Before visiting with the family, read everything you can about the case to extract the strengths, what they do well, and acknowledging where they were in life before coming to the attention of the agency. Remember to look for signs of socioeconomic status burdens that may have been reported as neglect due to unconscious bias or traditional mandated reporting versus mandated supporting. If you find yourself struggling to find strengths, you may want to assess if you are practicing social work through a narrow and uninformed lens. You may seek out a mentor or colleague who has a track record of family preservation and permanency.

When you arrive at the home, partner with the family and remind them of their many strengths. This will build rapport, trust, and empower the family. I once observed a mother walking form the trolley with her children in her arms, walking beside her, and in a stroller at 6am in the morning. When she arrived, she had at least an hour wait in the lobby. As she walked up to me to discuss her case, I began pondering how I could respond to her in a trauma-informed way recognizing what I have already observed. Her children were hungry, bored, and tired. Instead of greeting her with a hearty southern Good Morning!, I instead opted for, "It's been a rough morning hasn't it?" She let out a deep sigh, as her tense shoulders released some pressure. She then began to talk about how the children were giving her a run for her money. Then I said, "I saw how patient you were with your children, you're such a

great mother." She smiled, relaxed, and I believe her eyes
said to me, you "see" me. We both smiled at one another
and was able to wrap up the business of the day quickly.

I believe that small dose of trauma-informed
responsiveness made a difference. She would ask for me
personally whenever she visited the office after that. We
built a short-term relationship. You don't have to have 30
days or more to build a transformational relationship with a
family versus transactional. When working with families at
the office, don't look at it as if you're on opposite sides.
Realize that you too could be in that seat in the lobby.
We're not exempt.

8 BRING IN THE EXPERTS

Don't be too intimidated to Bring in the Experts.
Working with refugee families as well as Mexican Border
families was all new to me, so I needed to enlist the help of
the experts. People who know, understand, empathize with,
and are a part of the community and culture. Many of the
families I served were Ethiopian, Somalian, Cambodian,
Arab, etc. and I had never interacted with people from
those regions of the world. I was raised in the segregated
south through a western colonized lens. We did not share
religions, language, parenting styles, communication styles,
or even nonverbal cues. Although I believe I have the best
hospitality in the world, sometimes my authentic self was a
bit much for families. In my arsenal, I kept an open mind
and was willing to remove my western lens to take a look
through theirs.

So when you hear the story of a woman tying her
children to the bed to protect them from kidnapping, you
understand because she is transferring her homeland
context to this new world she lives in. You remind her of
how protective that action was and you work with her to
find safer methods of protection to prevent inadvertent
harm. The way you're able to communicate to her head and
her heart is to bring in the expert who understands and has
maybe even lived in that region of the world. This expert
acts as a doorway and conduit to building the bridge of
trust you need to create preservation and permanency for
this family.

"If you talk to a man in a language he understands, that
goes to his head. If you talk to him in his own language,
that goes to his heart." *Nelson Mandela*

9 INTRODUCE "YOU"

When you knock on the door, Introduce "YOU"! You'll have plenty of time to use your title, credentials, and badge. They know who you represent, but they don't know YOU! People pick up on disingenuous inauthenticity very well. The rest of your interview will go downhill from here if you fail to begin building trust at the onset. This may mean sharing things about yourself that you're comfortable revealing. I've shared that my mother was a teen mother, non-existent experience being a parent, and even that I have endured a divorce. Many times this helped to build common ground that I'm not showing up as if life has been perfect for me and lousy for them so we're so much different from one another. They begin to see me as a flawed human being and presume that I am less likely to judge them in their places of frailty.

Your "interview" and assessment should be more like a two-way conversation and you are collecting information along the way. Families mention many things when telling their life stories that are pertinent to the investigation. Each time I am ending the interview, families are offering me food or gifts. It was as pleasant of an experience as it could have been and I always want to leave them in better shape than what I found them in. So ask yourself, "Am I really interested in ensuring people know that they really matter, do I fulfill filling others cups"? That's what social work really is. So who are YOU, and are you proud enough in who you are to introduce YOU to families? If not, no worries, you just have some self-work to do!

10 VALIDATE BEST CHOICES

You will encounter cases where parents made a decision that was outside of the established norms. In those cases, learn to **Validate Best Choices.** Some parents are really given the choice of the lesser of two evils. Although the choice is not one you would promote or recommend, given certain circumstances try to put yourself in their shoes and think creatively what you would have done with their same resources. I received a case with a father who had an extensive record which included battery of a police office, past gang activity, and history of weapons in the home. As a new social worker standing 5'1 tall, I was asked if I wanted my 6'1 male colleague to join me or the police. I knew this would not set a great tone and decided I would use my social worker safety training skills and head out.

The man answered the door looking perturbed at me but soon we were in the kitchen and he was frying eggs for me and crying while telling me the story of what happened to his daughter. His daughter was involved in Commercial Sexual Exploitation of Children (CSEC). He stated that the police was not able to find his daughter so he began to search for her himself and found her with some men and proceeded to beat the men with a baseball bat. When the police arrived and tried to restrain him, he began swinging at them as well. I simply said, **"I understand why you made that choice in the protection and safety of your daughter."** He appreciated the validation and admitted that he knew it was wrong but was left with no other choice. It is imperative to note that during my practice as a social

worker and my overall 15 plus year social services career, I
have never experienced any harm from my clients. I do not
claim to be the best social worker; I believe the framework
of cultural humility and trauma informed practice provided
the best support.

Bonus-Practice Emotional Intelligence

Emotional Intelligence (EI/EQ) is your emotional quotient. It measures areas of aptitude when it comes to your emotions. There are four domains including, self-awareness, self-management, social awareness, and relationship management.

Self-awareness tells me that I have a very strong presence including my energy, the tone and pitch of my voice, as well as the personal space I take up. For some people, this may communicate aggression. This is nothing to be ashamed of, rather to be aware of and adjust as needed to ensure a successful interpersonal encounter and the building of a positive relationship.

Self-management helps me to monitor my reactions and responses to others actions and emotions. This means that I don't have to take anything personally and that others are not responsible for the way I choose to engage.

Social awareness assists me in being able to read others emotions through verbal and nonverbal cues.

Last, relationship management is the responsibility we take in ensuring that we are building positive connections with the people we engage with. Sometimes this means taking on our fair share of responsibility in the relationship and other times it means helping to support someone in the relationship that needs help carrying a heavier burden.

There are tests to find out how high or low you rate on the EI/EQ scale. Don't worry if it is low, you can work on it and get better. So in action my EQ could look like, lowering my voice, reducing eye contact, not responding negatively when met with negative feedback, watching for the other party's discomfort or fear, and last, taking accountability for something that is not my responsibility or obligation.

ABOUT THE AUTHOR

Dr. Keisha Clark is a native of New Orleans, La. and was evacuated to California in 2005 due to Hurricane Katrina. Growing up in the segregated south and experiencing a traumatic event uniquely positions her with lived experience expertise in cultural humility and trauma- informed practice. Dr. Clark's educational background includes an undergraduate degree earned at a Historically Black College and University (HBCU) in Psychology, a graduate degree in Criminal Justice, and a doctorate degree in Management with a concentration in Organizational Leadership. She currently leads the Office of Equity in San Diego County for Child Welfare Services. Her priorities are supporting the organization's efforts to become an antiracist system; tackling racial bias, disproportionality, disparities, inequities, diversity, inclusion, and belonging issues involving African Americans, Immigrants/Refugees, other communities of color as well as gender and sexual minorities (GSM). She has presented at Substance Abuse and Mental Health Services Administration (SAMHSA) national conferences advocating for African American, Hawaiian, and LGBT communities disproportionately affected by mental health and justice systems. She has provided consultation to develop transformational leadership, anti-racism, and mindfulness curriculum at San Diego City College, Emory University, and University of California San Diego (UCSD).

Dr. Clark has moderated racial justice listening sessions for
the California State Water Board, County of San Diego, and
the City of Imperial Beach, Ca. She has served as adjunct
faculty at Point Loma Nazarene University, Southwestern
Community College, San Diego State University, and
Indiana Wesleyan University teaching Criminology, Human
Services, Human Resources, and Psychology. Her passion
for equipping the next generation of social workers can be
observed through her strategic partnerships with Title IV E
programs including University of California Berkeley,
University of Texas Arlington, California State University
Fresno, and University of California, Davis. She is a
member of the Diversity & Inclusion Transformation
Team, co-chair of the Inclusion, Diversity, Equity, and
Anti-racism (IDEA) team and is a Justice, Equity, Diversity,
and Inclusion (JEDI) representative. In her spare time, Dr.
Clark enjoys being involved in volunteerism that promotes
community uplift and traveling.

Made in the USA
Las Vegas, NV
14 November 2023

80843817R00024